Origins
Shadow Swap

John Dougherty ■ Ishan Trivedi

OXFORD
UNIVERSITY PRESS

Chapter 1 – Grandma

Scott stood alone on the pavement, looking at his shadow. It stretched away from him, looking tall and thin in the low evening sunlight.

He scowled as he remembered what Grandma had said that morning: "He's scared of his own shadow, that one." It wasn't true. Of course it wasn't true; nobody was really scared of their own shadow. And she hadn't really meant it; she'd just meant that he got frightened easily.

He was frightened of lots of things, and he hated it. The dark, loud noises, heights, dogs, rats; all sorts of things scared him.

Most of all, he was scared of upsetting Grandma. He wished he didn't have to live with her. He wished he could live with his mum instead. But Mum had to work at three different jobs, so during the week he had to live with Grandma.

The trouble was, Grandma had no patience. She thought that playing was a silly waste of time. She was always too busy for him, and he never knew what would make her snap, or sigh, or roll her eyes.

As if his thoughts had come to life, suddenly another shadow moved over his own. He turned nervously to see Grandma looking at him.

"What are you doing hanging about out here, Scott? Haven't you got any homework to get on with?" Grandma said.

Scott could think of no answer that would have pleased her. He quietly slipped past his grandmother and made his way down the street towards the house. Glancing back nervously, he caught sight of his shadow again. It looked tall and confident, and for one strange second he envied it.

Perhaps that was why he had the dream that night – although given what happened afterwards, he found it difficult to believe it really was a dream.

Chapter 2 – Changing places

It was night. He was standing in the street, and every house was in complete darkness. The streetlights, too, were dead; it was as if the electricity had stopped flowing. Yet Scott could see quite clearly. The moon hung in the sky above him. It cast a strange brightness all around. And his shadow spread out in front of him.

Once more he envied his shadow. Nobody ever really noticed a shadow, though it was always there; nobody made it do anything. He thought of all the times he had wanted to fade into the background, so no one would notice him. It happened every day – in the playground, when they picked teams for football and left him out; in class, when the teacher set a homework he couldn't do; in shops, when he couldn't decide what to buy and felt the shopkeeper glaring at him … Most of all, it happened at home, when Grandma treated him as nothing more than a nuisance.

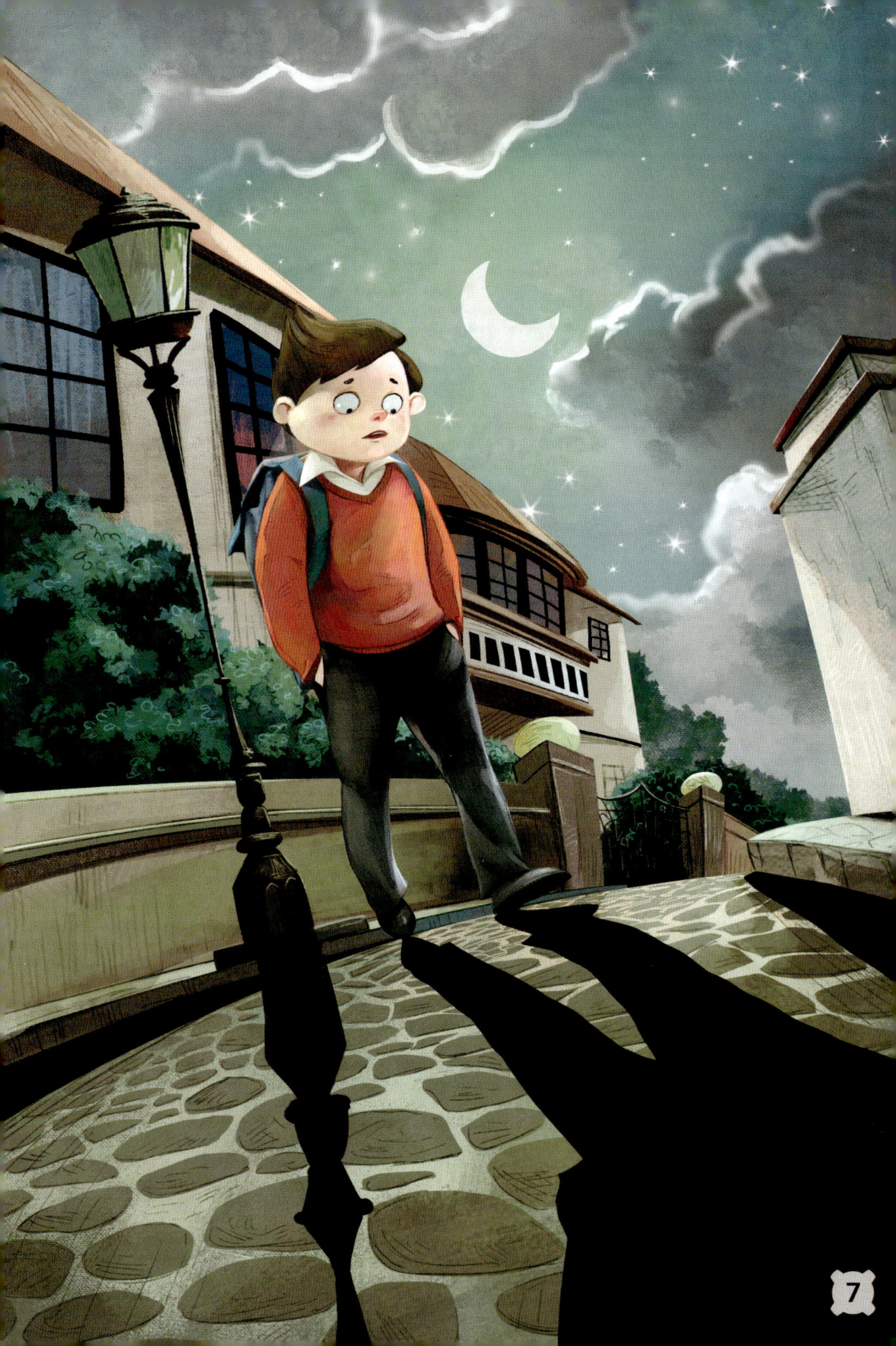

He looked again at his shadow in the moonlight.

"I wish I could be you," he murmured.

The moonlight seemed to grow brighter and bluer. A warm breeze sprang up. It whispered through the bare branches of a little tree, and rustled the dry, fallen leaves on the pavement.

And the shadow murmured back, "Are you sure?"

Scott's head was drowsy in this dream world. It seemed quite normal that his shadow should talk to him.

"Yes," he answered softly. "I'm sure."

"Then run," said the shadow.

Scott ran.

His feet lifted from the pavement, feeling lighter than ever before, and his shadow ran with him. It felt as if the moonlight was giving him wings; as if he could run forever and never grow tired. Faster and faster he ran; for one joyful moment he almost believed he was going to outrun his shadow and leave it behind.

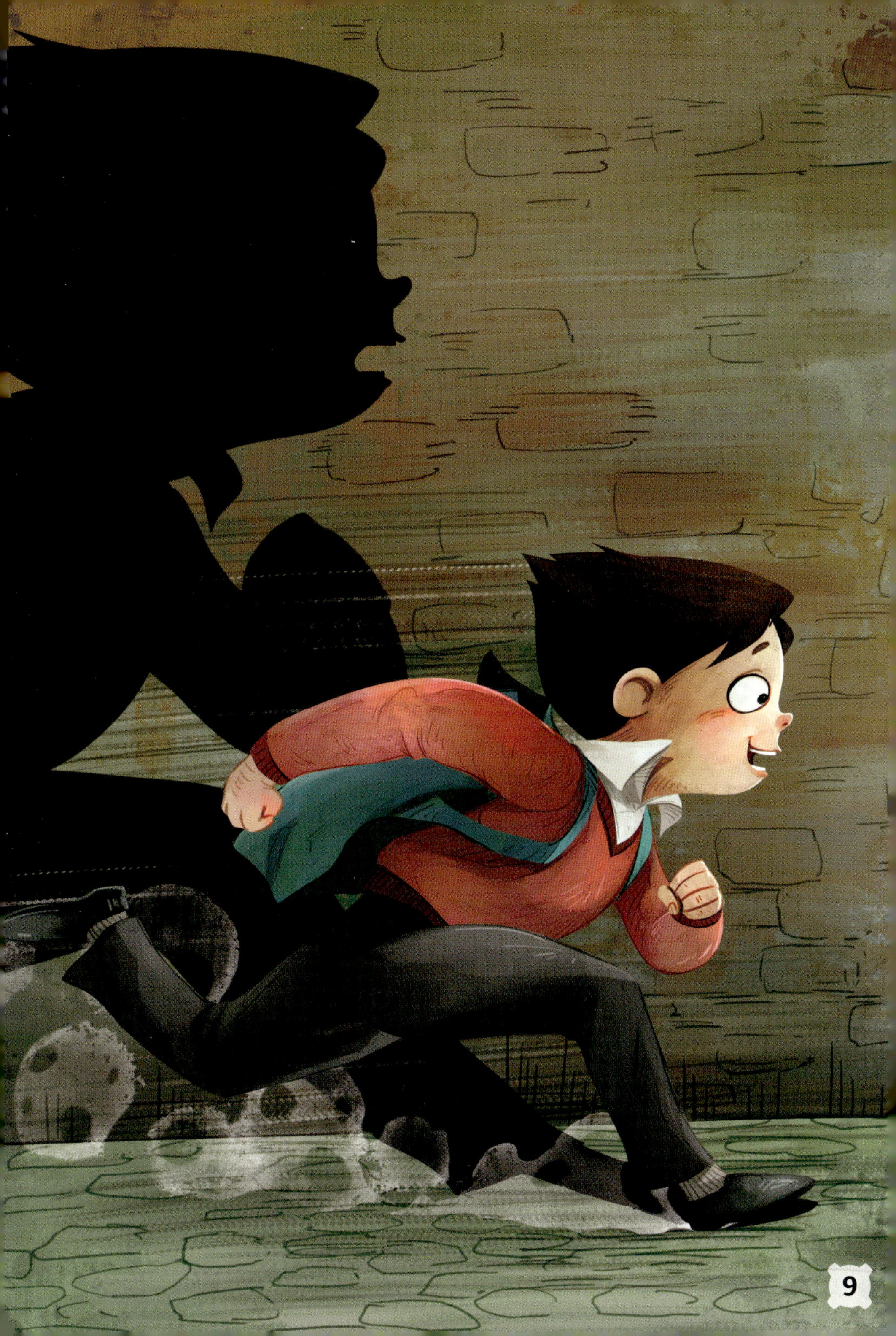

Then he felt a drag, a weight, like water flowing around his feet. It was as if something was clinging to his shoes. He pressed on, trying to run faster, but the weight was growing. Still running, he looked down.

As Scott ran, his shadow started to grow upwards from the ground. Its feet were still moving with his, its arms pounding, but it rose upright. Suddenly, Scott found himself running to keep up with it. Yet the shadow kept running faster. Scott felt himself losing his balance, falling backwards …

Chapter 3 – Life as a shadow

When he woke, the sun was streaming through the windows of his bedroom. *Just a dream,* he thought. *It was just a dream.*

It took him a moment to realize that something was lying on top of him. Something large, and dark.

It took him another moment to realize that it was his shadow.

Scott tried to push the shadow off him and found he couldn't. It was solid and heavy. And he was flat. There was no other word for it. He was flat. Flat as a pancake, flat as a well-ironed t-shirt. And his shadow was not.

The shadow stirred, stretched, sat up and bounded out of bed. "Morning!" it said cheerfully, looking down at Scott.

It didn't have a face, but Scott somehow knew it was smiling. He tried to peel himself from the bed, but it was no use. "What have you done to me?" he asked.

The shadow shrugged. "I didn't do anything," he said. "You did it to yourself. You decided it was easier to shrink into the background and let me do the living."

Again, Scott somehow knew that it was smiling, and smiling broadly. "And I'm going to! I've been stuck to your ankles way too long. It's my turn to have fun, and your turn to be the shadow!"

The shadow turned and opened the bedroom door, and Scott felt himself sliding off the bed after it. Then he slipped onto the floor, out of the room and – rather bumpily, though not painfully – down the stairs.

It was a sunny day, but the morning sun didn't shine into the kitchen. Scott felt himself fading as the shadow sat down and began to gobble up his breakfast.

Grandma, busy cooking, glanced at the shadow. "You look a bit grubby, Scott," she sighed. "When did you last have a bath?"

"Saturday," the shadow answered cheerfully. "Did you sleep well, Grandma?"

Grandma shook her head. "No, I didn't, since you ask," she said, scrubbing angrily at a frying pan. "Right: I want you to have a bath this evening."

Her tone was sharp and impatient, but instead of putting its head down, as Scott would have done, the shadow just nodded. "Okay, Grandma," it said.

Scott suddenly felt jealous of his shadow again. Why couldn't he talk to Grandma like that? Just a word, just a sigh from her was enough to make him feel small. Yet the shadow seemed to deal with it so well.

"Better go," the shadow said, standing up. "Don't want to be late!"

Scott felt himself sliding along the floor and out into the hallway. The shadow picked up his schoolbag and made for the door.

Chapter 4 – The football match

Outside, in the bright sunlight, Scott felt himself suddenly visible again. He wasn't sure he liked it. He'd been happy that Grandma couldn't see him at breakfast time. It felt good when no one noticed him. But he had a question.

"Um … shadow," he said quietly. Then louder. "Shadow?"

The shadow stopped, and looked down at him. "Sorry, did you say something?"

"Er … yeah, I just wondered. How come Grandma didn't notice that you're a shadow? And I'm flat, but I'm still me. How come she didn't see me on the wall behind you?"

Again, he got the feeling that the shadow was smiling. "Grandma doesn't see me as a shadow because I'm not acting like a shadow."

Before Scott could ask what it meant, the shadow broke into a run, and he felt himself sliding along the pavement. He glided over bumps and drain covers, over fallen leaves and loose pebbles. It felt strange, but pleasant – a bit like being tickled and a bit like being stroked. It was almost like being a bird, he thought – or a boat skimming over the waves. He felt himself flickering through railings; leaping onto parked cars, and off again. It felt new; it felt different; it felt good.

It felt less good once he arrived at school. The playground was full of people, and they all seemed to be stepping on his face.

Of course, when a foot landed on him, it didn't hurt. He quickly realized it was impossible for anyone to actually step on him; if a foot landed where his face was, a foot-shaped part of his face would pop onto the shoe and stay there until the shoe moved off. But he didn't like it. It felt weird. It felt uncomfortable. And there was worse to come.

Scott usually played football, but only because all the other boys in the class did. He never enjoyed it, because the others always made him go in goal. Always. He hated being in goal. It was boring most of the time, and when it wasn't boring it was terrifying. The others had learned that the easiest way to score was to kick the ball directly at his face. They knew he'd duck.

"Don't," he said, as the shadow ran into the middle of the football match.

The shadow ignored him. "Which team am I on?" it asked.

Toby and Josh, team captains as usual, looked at each other and shrugged. "Mine, I suppose," Josh said. "You can be in goal."

"I was in goal yesterday," the shadow said, and Scott felt his heart sink.

"I said, you're in goal," Josh repeated.

Scott knew what would happen next. The shadow would say that wasn't fair; Josh would shrug and say if he wanted to play he'd have to go in goal; everyone else would back Josh up; and that would be it.

But the shadow had other ideas. "No," it repeated, "I went in goal yesterday. I'll play midfield today."

Josh pushed the shadow, hard. The shadow staggered back, taking Scott with it.

21

Scott felt a kick of fear in his chest, but the shadow just sighed and said, "Look, we don't have long till the bell goes. Can we just get on with the game?"

"We can get on with the game when you get in goal," Josh insisted.

"We can get on with the game now," the shadow said calmly.

There was a pause. Several of the others glared at the shadow.

And then Toby said, "Come on, Josh. Let's just play."

"I don't mind going in goal," said someone else.

There was a pause. "OK then," said Josh. He scowled at the shadow. "But you're in goal next time," he said.

The shadow didn't exactly ignore him, but it didn't agree, either. It just shrugged and stood ready to join in the game.

And what a game it was. The shadow wasn't a particularly good player, but it tried its best, and the result was – well, it was fun. For the shadow, at least.

23

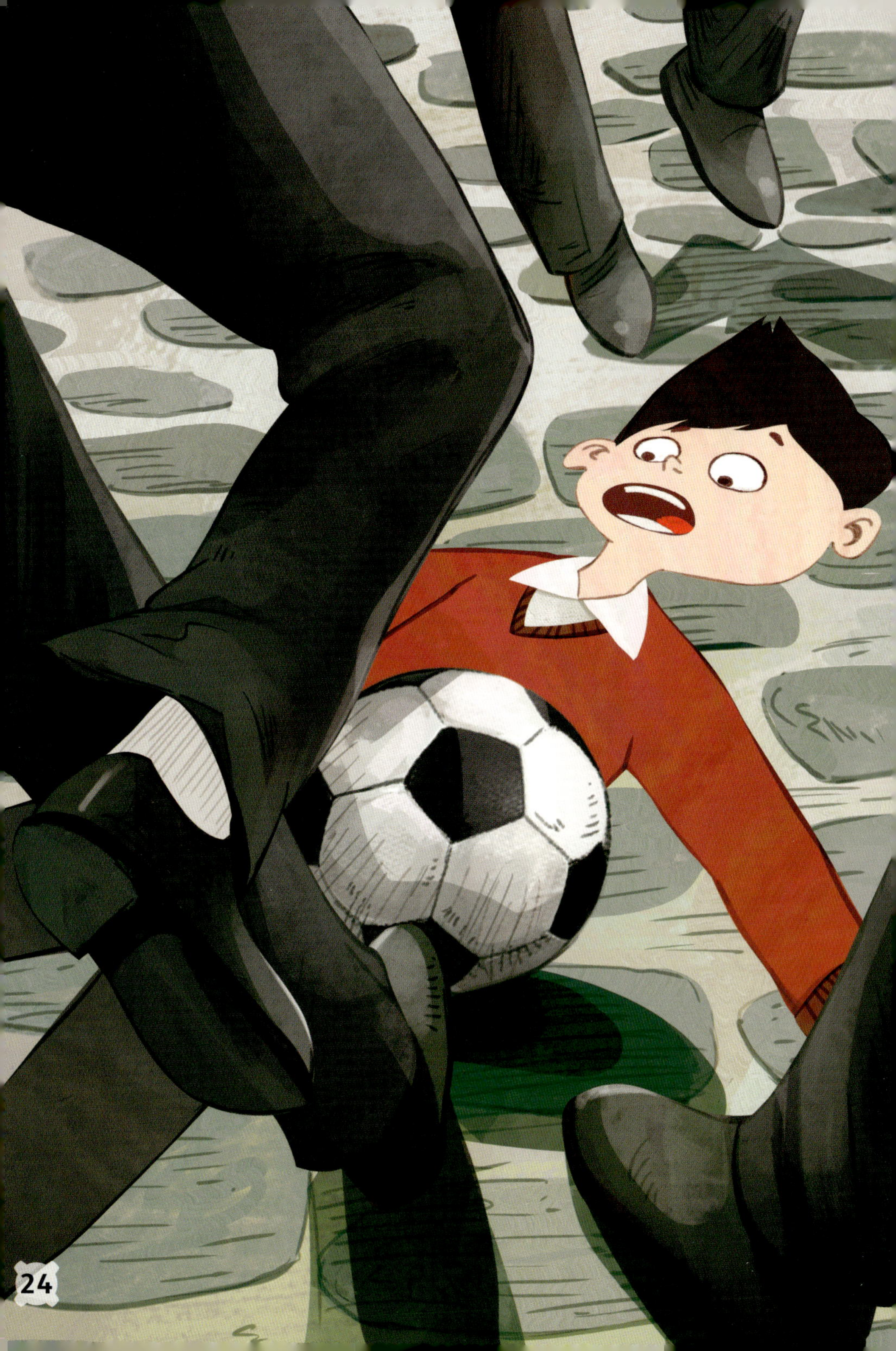

It wasn't so much fun for Scott. He was dragged across the playground, through the other players and across the ball. The longer it went on, the less he enjoyed it.

In the classroom, later, he realized why. He quite liked not being noticed, but he didn't enjoy having no choice. Whatever the shadow wanted to do, it did, and Scott was just pulled along behind it.

It was everything he hated about his own life, but worse. In day-to-day life, everybody bossed him around. Nobody let him be who he was or do what he wanted; nobody listened to him.

Now, as a shadow, it was as if he wasn't even there. He had no choice except to trail along behind the shadow, stuck to its heels. He followed it out to play, and back in again; it towed him to lunch, and at the end of the day, it dragged him home.

Chapter 5 – Taking control

The shadow stopped outside Grandma's house, and looked down at Scott. He looked back at the shadow. And although he felt somehow nervous, he found his voice. "I want to change back," he said.

The shadow looked down at him, and shook its head. "I like your life," it said. "And I think I'm living it better than you do."

It turned away, as if the conversation was over. Normally, when someone did that, Scott just gave in. He felt as if he had no choice and no right to speak up. But now he suddenly realized that if he didn't want to spend the rest of his life as a shadow, he needed to speak up for himself.

27

"No," he said, in a clear voice. "It's *my* life. You can't have it."

The shadow looked down in surprise. "But you said you wanted to change places. You said you were sure."

"Yes," Scott agreed. "I did want to change places, but now it's time to change back. It's *my* life, and you can't have it."

The shadow shook its head again, and turned as if to go. But Scott had learned from what had happened today. He had seen how the shadow had stood up for itself, calmly and without shouting. He had seen how it had pushed for what was fair. "It's *my* life," he repeated. "*You* can't have it."

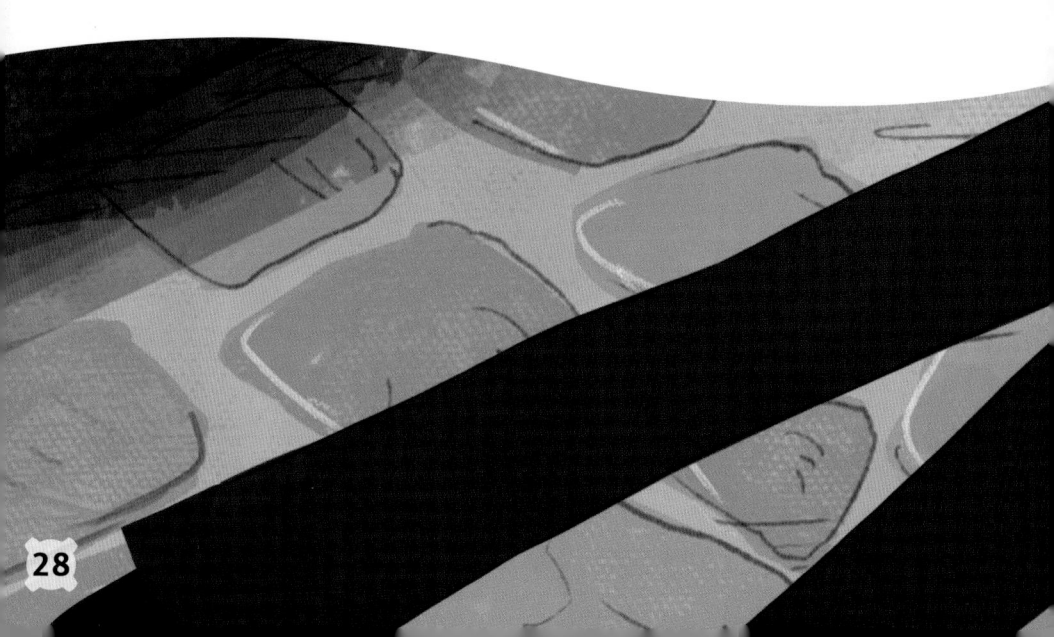

29

As he said the words, he felt them to be true. It was *his* life, and he wasn't going to let anyone else treat him like a shadow, and step on him. "You can't have it," he said again, calmly and firmly. He suddenly felt himself growing, peeling from the pavement. He was solid again now, and he rose up until he was standing nose to nose with the shadow. "It's *my* life," he repeated.

The shadow's face was smooth and blank, but somehow Scott felt again that it was smiling.

"It is," the shadow agreed. "It's your life. And if you can live it – live it properly, live it well, so that you enjoy it – I'm happy to be your shadow."

And it shrank back down and flattened itself against the pavement, an ordinary shadow once more.

Scott looked down at it and smiled to himself. Just at that moment, his shadow was covered by another.

He turned, to see Grandma.

"Well?" she said.

Scott hesitated, feeling that old nervousness returning. And then he remembered what he'd learned that day, and smiled up at her. "I'm very well, thanks, Grandma," he said. "How are you? Have you had a good day?"

And to his surprise, Grandma smiled back.